MY HAMSTER

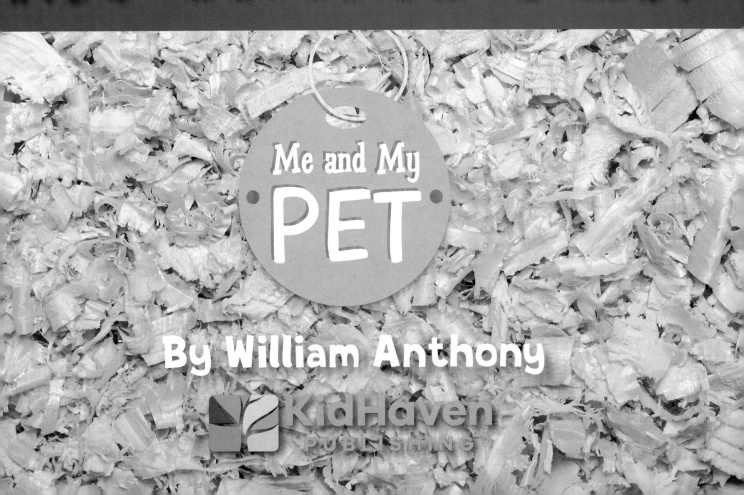

Me and My
PET

By William Anthony

KidHaven
PUBLISHING

Published in 2020 by KidHaven Publishing, an Imprint of Greenhaven Publishing, LLC
353 3rd Avenue, Suite 255, New York, NY 10010

This edition is published by arrangement with Booklife Publishing.

Written by: William Anthony
Edited by: Robin Twiddy
Designed by: Jasmine Pointer

Cataloging-in-Publication Data

Names: Anthony, William.
Title: My hamster / William Anthony.
Description: New York : KidHaven Publishing, 2020. | Series: Me and my pet | Includes glossary and index.
Identifiers: ISBN 9781534533493 (pbk.) | ISBN 9781534533516 (library bound) | ISBN 9781534533509 (6 pack) | ISBN 9781534533523 (ebook)
Subjects: LCSH: Hamsters as pets--Juvenile literature.
Classification: LCC SF459.H3 A58 2020 | DDC 636.935'6--dc23

Photo credits: Images are courtesy of Shutterstock.com. With thanks to Getty Images, Thinkstock Photo and IStockphoto.
Front cover - Max Topchii, Guas. 2 - Ilyashenko Oleksiy. 3 - Billion Photos, KanzBoo. 4 & 5 - Max Topchii. 6 - floorAleks. 7 - honzy. 8 - Nomad_Soul,
AtiwatPhotography. 9 - dwori. 10 - AtiwatPhotography. 11 - Victoria Rak, Adrin Shamsudin. 13 - fantom_rd. 14 - ANKorr. 15 - Montree Sanyos.
16 - santypan. 17 - santypan. 18 - . Phiwath Wittayawatn . 19 - Organic Matter. 20 - stock_shot. 21 - tanya_izz. 22 - Max Topchii. 23 - ChompooSuppa.

Printed in the United States of America

CPSIA compliance information: Batch #BW20KL. For further information contact Greenhaven Publishing LLC, New York, New York at 1-844-317-7404.

CONTENTS

Words that look like **this** can be found in the glossary on page 24.

Heidi ♥ and Sandy

Heidi

Sandy

Hello! My name's Heidi, and this is my pet hamster, Sandy. She's eight months old. Hamsters are my favorite animal because they're really cute and easy to look after!

4

Whether you're thinking about getting one, or you've had one for a little while, Sandy and I are going to take you through how to look after a hamster!

Lead the way, Sandy!

Getting a Hamster

Getting a hamster to look after means you are going to have a lot of **responsibility**. You will need to feed them and give them a nice home with lots of toys.

My family got Sandy from a pet store, but you can also get a hamster from other places. You can get a hamster from someone who **breeds** them.

Always make sure you research the person or place you're buying a pet from.

Home

Put a layer of wood flakes on the bottom of the cage for them, like a little carpet!

Hamsters are very small, so they don't need lots of space. You will need to get them a cage to live in, with bedding and places to exercise.

It is important to give hamsters lots of things to play with in their cage. They need plenty of things to play with or they will get bored – just like you!

Hamsters like climbing through tubes and running on hamster wheels!

Playtime

You need to help your hamster get used to being held by people. Try letting them run over your hand before gently trying to hold them.

It's also fun for your hamster to explore outside their cage. You can put them in a hamster ball so you don't lose them when they're running around!

Food

Hamsters need food to stay alive, just like we do. Hamster food is easy to buy and prepare. You can get it from any pet store. You just need to put it in a little bowl.

Make sure you also fill up their water bottle!

It's good to give your hamster other things to eat as well, such as small chunks of carrot, cucumber, or apple. This gives them a **diet** that is nice and **varied**.

Bedtime

Hamsters are crepuscular (say: creh-puss-cue-ler), which means they sleep during the daytime and wake up in the evenings and mornings.

ZZzzz!

To help your hamster sleep well, you should give them
a little sleeping area. Fill it with lots of soft bedding
or **shredded** paper to keep them comfortable!

15

The Vet

Vets are doctors, but for animals instead of humans!

Hamsters can get sick, just like humans. Hamsters that are sick can go see the vet. The vet will do everything they can to help your hamster get better again!

One evening, Sandy didn't come out of her bedding to play. I told my parents and we took her to the vet, who made her all better again!

If you think your hamster isn't very well, make sure you tell someone.

Growing Up

Hamsters have quite a short life, and they start getting old just before they are two years old. You might notice them start to lose their hair or exercise less.

It is important to be very gentle with an old hamster. Stroke and pet them softly, and be very calm around them.

Super Hamsters

Hamsters can do some amazing things, but a lot of those things are very strange! Hamsters can store so much food in their cheeks that it can double their weight!

Don't try this at home — we can't see what's behind us!

Did you know that hamsters can also run backward just as quickly as they run forward? In the wild, this helps them to quickly escape tunnels if there is an **intruder** coming!

You and Your Pet

So, whether you've got your super hamster already or you're thinking of getting one, make sure you take care of them just like Sandy and I have taught you!

I'm sure you'll make a great pet owner. Try to think of some cool toys you can put in your hamster's cage, and most of all, enjoy your new fluffball!

GLOSSARY

breed — to take care of animals in order to make more animals

diet — the kinds of food that an animal or person usually eats

intruder — something that is not welcome or should not be in a place

research — to gather information about a subject

responsibility — having tasks that you are expected to do

shredded — when a material is cut into long, thin strips

varied — mixed from different things

INDEX

24